DWIGHT GOODEN

THE ACHIEVERS

DWIGHT GOODEN

Strikeout King

Nathan Aaseng

Lerner Publications Company ▪ Minneapolis

This book is available in two editions:
Library binding by Lerner Publications Company
Soft cover by First Avenue Editions
241 First Avenue North
Minneapolis, Minnesota 55401

To William Bates

LIBRARY OF CONGRESS CATALOGING-IN-PUBLICATION DATA

Aaseng, Nathan.
  Dwight Gooden : strikeout king.

  (The Achievers)
  Summary: A biography with emphasis on the career of
the record-making pitcher for the New York Mets.
  1. Gooden, Dwight — Juvenile literature. 2. Baseball
players — United States — Biography — Juvenile literature.
3. Pitching (Baseball) — Juvenile literature. [1. Gooden,
Dwight. 2. Baseball players. 3. Afro-American — Biography]
I. Title. II. Series.
GV865.G62A63   1988 796.357′092′4 [B] [92] 87-4072
ISBN 0-8225-0478-2 (lib. bdg.)
ISBN 0-8225-9549-4 (pbk.)

Manufactured in the United States of America

International Standard Book Number: 0-8225-0478-2 (lib. bdg.)
International Standard Book Number: 0-8225-9549-4 (pbk.)
Library of Congress Catalog Card Number: 87-4072

6 7 8 9 10 98 97 96 95 94 93

DWIGHT GOODEN

Strikeout King

The kind of news that shakes up a ballplayer's life had just been broken to New York Mets shortstop Hubie Brooks. As of that day—December 10, 1984— Brooks was no longer a Met. He had been traded to the Montreal Expos for All-Star catcher Gary Carter. Brooks groaned at the thought of the troubles the swap would bring. But it wasn't the inconvenience of moving to a new city or the sadness of leaving old friends that bothered him the most. Being traded by the Mets meant something far more dismal for his future. "Oh, no!" he moaned. "Now I have to face Dwight!"

An effortless pitching motion disguises the fact that Gooden's fastball will arrive at the plate traveling at 96 miles per hour.

Meanwhile, the veteran Gary Carter accepted the news that his 10-year stay with the Expos had ended. When asked what he liked about the trade, Carter smiled as if a sliver that had been bothering him for months had suddenly been removed. The best thing, he said, was that he "wouldn't have to hit against Doc anymore."

It was no coincidence that Carter and Brooks were thinking of the same person. Dwight "Dr. K" Gooden of the New York Mets weighed heavily on the minds of all National League hitters in 1984 — so heavily that not even a stunning trade could push him out of their thoughts. Dwight Gooden was not just a pitcher or not just the best pitcher in baseball. He was "The Force." Doc Gooden could fire a 96-mile-per-hour fastball with no more effort than if he were tossing a dart. His curve ball snapped into the catcher's mitt at 80 miles per hour, faster than some pitchers' fastballs. In the words of former Met teammate Wally Backman, a batter "couldn't hit that pitch with a four-by-four!" Gooden had such splendid control that, unlike most power pitchers, he could "paint the corners of the plate" with both the curve and the fastball all game long. To make matters worse for hitters, Dwight never seemed to get rattled, and he seemed to know what he wanted to do with each pitch.

Impressive as all these talents were, what really scared batters was Gooden's birth certificate. The records showed that Dwight Gooden was born on November 16, 1964. That meant the pitcher who was tying them up in knots was just a 19-year-old kid. Awesome as he was, Gooden was only feeling his way around the league, trying to pick up some experience.

Among his many nicknames, Dwight Gooden could have added, "The Youngest." Sportswriters hardly ever mentioned his name without adding, "the youngest pitcher ever to...." Record keepers pronounced him the youngest pitcher ever to play in an All-Star game and the youngest pitcher to be named Rookie of the

Met owner Nelson Doubleday congratulates Dwight on winning the 1984 National League Rookie of the Year Award. Three other Mets—Tom Seaver (1967), Jon Matlack (1972), and Darryl Strawberry (1983)—received the award previously.

Year. In 1985, he became the youngest ever to win 20 games and the youngest to win the Cy Young Award, which honors the league's top pitcher.

As frightening as the present Dwight Gooden was, the thought of the future Dwight Gooden was even more terrifying. Most pitchers didn't reach their peak until their late 20s, so National League batters could not block the question from their minds. What was Dr. K going to be like when he hit that peak? No less an expert than Sandy Koufax, the Los Angeles Dodgers' legendary, flame-throwing lefty, said, "I wouldn't trade anyone's past for Dwight's future."

By Dwight's third season, however, many Met fans were wondering if the promise of a Hall of Fame career had been a lie. While the Mets were romping to an easy National League East title in 1986, everyone's favorite question seemed to be "What's wrong with Doc?" Although he was still posting All-Star-level statistics, something seemed to be missing. The pressure of living up to superhuman standards seemed to have drained Dwight by the end of the year. The Mets, whom Dwight had almost single-handedly carried through the pennant fight in 1985, won the 1986 World Series without a single post-season victory from their ace.

Then came a nightmarish off-season that began with a fight with the Tampa, Florida, police and ended with stunning evidence of cocaine use. Gooden's once-certain future was clouded in doubt. Which was he: the fabulous Dr. K, the best pitching prospect ever, or just plain Dwight Gooden, another flash in the pan who couldn't handle success?

Dan Gooden would have been happy making baseball his life. Fate, however, seemed determined to keep that from happening. A severe case of arthritis hampered his efforts as a first baseman for the semi-pro Albany Red Sox and, at the age of 26, forced Dwight's father to take his .280 batting average into retirement. Gooden then turned to coaching in the Tampa area, hoping that his children could take up where his aching joints had been forced to leave off.

Baseball seemed to run in the Gooden family. Many years earlier, Grandpa Uclessee Gooden had carved out a reputation for himself on the Georgia sandlots with his blistering fastball. But none of Dan's three sons from his first marriage seemed interested in carrying on the old tradition, nor did his two daughters. It wasn't until 11 years after the birth of his fifth child that Dwight came along. Once again, Dan Gooden carried a son around with him at his ball games, just as his father had once carried him. This time, however, it turned out to be more than just baby-sitting. At long last, Dan Gooden had his wish: a child who soaked up the baseball scene like a sponge.

At the age of three, young Dwight would toss a ball to his father's players, and they would patiently roll it back to him. When "nuisances" such as meals and bedtime kept him away from the ball park, Dwight tried to take the game with him. While in bed, he would toss a tennis ball in the air and catch it until finally dozing off.

The next morning, Dwight would race outside to take "batting practice." Since he didn't have any balls suitable for whacking so close to houses, he used crushed soda cans. Pretending to be a big-league star, Dwight pounded soda cans and sometimes had to climb on the roof to retrieve the few he had hit too hard. The noise might have gotten him in trouble in some neighborhoods, but the Goodens lived in a close-knit working class community. Dwight later remembered that "all the adults seemed like parents" to him. Rather than getting upset when Dwight's early morning can-whacking repeatedly awoke him, an older man who lived across the street called Dwight's practice his wake-up call.

When Dwight was six, his father took him to nearby Lakeland, the spring training headquarters of the Detroit Tigers. There he saw Tiger outfielder Al Kaline blast two home runs in an exhibition game. The sight of one player totally taking charge of a game thrilled him. From that moment, Al Kaline was Dwight's hero, and he set out to follow in his steps.

Although Detroit Tiger right fielder Al Kaline won only one batting crown and never led the league in home runs, his all-around skills made him Gooden's favorite player.

When Dwight couldn't be knocking cans or balls around, he would try his hand at pitching and challenge his friend Floyd Youmans to pitching contests. They threw balls against brick walls, choosing certain bricks as the strike zone and trying to see who could throw the most strikes. Even though they had been warned that curveballs were very hard on young arms, Floyd and Dwight would still sneak in a few.

It was the Goodens' good fortune to live in a neighborhood that offered a Little League program nationally famous for its success. Started after a series of riots in 1967 to give kids something constructive to do, the teams had always done well in national competition. When Dwight joined the League at the age of 10, the competition nearly choked off his interest in the game. Now the boy who had been frustrated because he was always so much better in baseball than his friends suddenly found himself on the other side of the fence. In his first five at-bats, Dwight went hitless and struck out three times. He was ready to quit, but a long talk with his dad helped to straighten him out. That wouldn't be the last time Dan Gooden would come to his son's rescue.

Quickly, Dwight turned things around and became a star outfielder for his team. The coaches noticed his powerful arm, however, and brought him in to play third base, where he could put that arm to better use. The next step was to put it to even better use—as a pitcher. At the age of 12, Dwight resigned himself to the fact that he wasn't going to roam the outfield like Al Kaline. Instead, he reluctantly concentrated on making the most of his extraordinary pitching skills. He had not, however, given up his fascination with players who could dominate a game. His new heroes were overpowering strikeout pitchers such as Nolan Ryan and J. R. Richard.

Gooden threw so hard almost no one could catch his pitches, and those who tried ran the risk of breaking their hand or wrist. Baseball history, however, is filled with tales of young men with cannon arms who never made it in the pros. What made Gooden unique was his control. Even such fastball legends as "Rapid" Robert Feller and Sandy Koufax spent several years in the major leagues before their pitches found the plate. From the start, Dwight's pitches were not scatter-shot missiles but precision bullets. Floyd Youmans could tell that Dwight was something special. "At the age of 12, I knew he had command," he later marveled.

Dwight's teammates also picked up on the way Gooden could skillfully disarm a batter. "Come on, Doctor, operate on this guy," they would chatter as Dwight prepared to face the next hitter. That, along with Gooden's admiration of basketball star Julius "Dr. J" Erving, eventually earned him the nickname of "Doc."

Once it became obvious that he could not escape a pitching career, Gooden switched his allegiance from sluggers such as Kaline to power pitchers like all-time strikeout leader Nolan Ryan.

Most hard throwers such as Hall of Famer Sandy Koufax struggled in the major leagues before gaining control of their pitches. Gooden, however, mastered his pitching while still a teenager.

It took Dwight a long time to get used to the fact he was several notches above the average Little League player. According to his dad, Dwight could play so well he couldn't understand the failings of others. Occasionally, a teammate would botch what Dwight considered an easy play. Not only was Dwight critical of those mistakes, he sometimes became so frustrated he would quit the game. Finally, his dad put a stop to it. "Just play your position," he scolded. "Quit once more and you quit for good!"

Gooden's temper continued to cause problems for him in junior high. Because Dwight's fastball so over-powered his opponents that just getting a foul ball off him was considered a victory, it became easy for him to think he should get everyone out. In one game, however, several hitters proved that Dwight was only human by slashing solid hits off him. Furious with himself, Dwight slammed his fist against a wall and hurt his hand. His pain helped to reinforce lessons that Dwight's mom was trying to teach him. While he gives his dad all of the credit for his baseball development, Dwight credits his mother, Ella Mae, with improving his attitude. It was she who finally convinced her son that his temper was only hurting him and making him look foolish.

As a ninth grader, Dwight didn't see much hope of playing regularly on the Hillsborough High School team that was loaded with seniors and juniors. At the same time, the family was facing a tough period when his father's arthritis forced him to give up his job. For the next two seasons, Dwight spent more time at home and left the high school ball diamond to the older kids.

By the time he reported to the squad in his junior year, Dwight had matured dramatically. The temperamental star of Little League had disappeared and, left

Dwight (back row, far right) poses with the other members of his high school team.

in its place, was a model of patience and self-control. Dwight's former coaches must have done a double take when a high school coach described him as a selfless team player who never argued or lost his temper.

After perfecting the new methods of gripping the ball that his coach, Billy Reed, had shown him, Gooden blew away opposing batters. Thanks to the new grips, his pitches dipped and sailed instead of flying toward the plate in a straight groove. During his senior year at Hillsborough, Dwight's fielders must have felt as though they were out in the field just for show. Gooden struck out 130 batters in 74 innings that year, including one perfect game (no hits and no walks).

While that kind of pitching attracted pro scouts, no one suggested that Dwight was any kind of superman. Even the New York Mets, who scouted him closely, didn't rate him at the top of their list of prospects. No one, then, was more shocked than Dwight to hear the Mets had used their first-round choice to select him in the 1982 draft of amateur players. Not believing he could have been the fifth player chosen in the entire draft, Dwight even called New York to make sure there hadn't been some mistake. Then he must have really thought he was dreaming when he heard the Mets had taken his friend Floyd Youmans in the second round.

After signing with New York in June of 1982, Dwight reported to the Mets' Kingsport, Tennessee, club in the Appalachian Rookie League. Even though he was

It was Dad's turn to look over Dwight's shoulder as he signed a long-term contract with the New York Mets.

far more fortunate than most rookies in having a good friend, Youmans, playing with him, Gooden felt uneasy stepping outside the cozy surroundings of his Belmont Heights neighborhood. For the baby of the family who had been always watched over by adoring older sisters, life on his own was a hard adjustment. Gooden survived by phoning home at least once—and often twice—a day.

While at Kingsport, Gooden cranked up his one-two punch—the blazing fastball and the sweeping curve— to strike out 66 batters in 66 innings. He finished out the year at the Mets' farm club in Little Falls, New York.

The Mets received a double dose of Tampa heat when Gooden's flame-throwing friend, Floyd Youmans, also joined the team in 1982. Ironically, Youmans first broke out of Gooden's shadow as a part of the trade that brought Gary Carter to the Mets.

While it may have seemed he was stuck out in the middle of nowhere, at least one important person was watching Dwight's strikeouts. Dave Johnson, ex-second baseman for the Baltimore Orioles and the Atlanta Braves, had signed on as a coach in the Mets' minor-league system. A veteran of 13 seasons in the majors, Johnson had seen just about everything in baseball. But he had never seen anything like the pitches hurtling toward the plate from the hand of Dwight Gooden. As Johnson moved higher in the Mets' organization, he was convinced that in Gooden the team had "the best prospect I ever saw."

In 1983, the secret of Dwight Gooden's talent exploded out of the backwaters of the Mets' minor-league system. Moving up to tougher competition in Lynchburg, Virginia, Gooden shattered a long-standing minor-league record for strikeouts. Back in 1947, a pitcher named Ken Deal had fanned 275 batters, and not before or since had a minor-league pitcher struck out as many. Now Doc Gooden breezed past that mark and owned 286 strikeouts with one game to go.

Usually, Dwight did not worry about striking out batters and always claimed he would rather get a groundout or a pop-up so he wouldn't have to throw so many pitches. But the thought of boosting the record to an even 300 set his mouth watering. Trying for strikeouts in every inning, Dwight whiffed 14 batters in a seven-inning game to reach his goal.

The media took plenty of pictures of the Mets' new sensation, but they recorded few of his words as the team protected him from the constant demands for interviews.

That left him with a record of 300 strikeouts in only 191 innings to go with his 19-4 won-lost mark.

Despite his success, Gooden was in no rush to get to the majors. His dad figured if Dwight were patient and worked hard, he would probably get a shot at the Mets in 1986. So when Gooden was issued a last-minute invitation to join the Mets' spring training camp in 1984, he guessed he was only getting a chance to gain some experience.

The Mets, however, had found themselves with an unexpected opening on their roster. During the off-season, their veteran starting pitcher, Tom Seaver, had been left unprotected in a player compensation pool. Since Seaver was nearing the end of his career and commanded a huge salary, they were certain no team would claim him. But the Chicago White Sox had, and, without their top pitcher, the last-place Mets suddenly found their situation even grimmer.

The 19-year-old Gooden was still all set to pack his bags after the team's final exhibition game when the Mets' new manager walked up to him and said, "Congratulations!" The new manager was Dave Johnson, who had first seen Dwight play in Little Falls. Johnson had vowed then that, if it were up to him, the kid would be his starting pitcher, no matter the level of competition. Had Gooden known of Johnson's intent, he would not have been so stunned to find himself a Met two years ahead of his father's prediction.

A miscalculation by the Mets' management cost them the services of star pitcher Tom Seaver and opened the door for Gooden's early arrival in the majors.

Johnson knew the chance he was taking in moving Dwight. Many young, golden arms ended up in the scrap pile because they had been pushed into the majors too soon. He remembered a young Met pitcher named Tim Leary who had been able to pump a fastball as hard as Gooden could. New York had sent

Tempting as it was to use Gooden's talents to the maximum, Met manager Dave Johnson carefully rationed Dwight's innings.

Leary to the mound on a cold April day. The rookie hurt his arm while pitching that game and never again showed the promise of his earlier days.

With that memory in mind, Johnson chose to break in his new star carefully. He did not send Gooden to the mound until April 7 when the Mets played indoors in the climate-controlled air of Houston's Astrodome. The Astrodome had the added advantage of being a "pitcher's park," a roomy field where long fly balls fell for outs instead of home runs.

Still not quite believing he was pitching in the big leagues, Gooden nervously walked out to the mound. He had always been a thinking pitcher who knew what type of pitch he wanted to throw to each batter. But this time, he was so rattled he forgot everything he knew about pitching. Gooden just fired the ball towards the plate and waited for something to happen.

As it turned out, very little happened. The Houston Astros managed only one run off Dwight in five innings, with five of them called out on strikes. Careful to protect his young star's arm from too much strain, manager Johnson took him out after five innings and let the Mets' bullpen protect his first major-league win. Throughout his early years, the Mets continued to watch Gooden's innings more closely than a dieter watches calories. They would not risk letting him throw too many pitches in a game, and they made certain he had at least four days' rest between starts.

The Mets didn't believe in totally sheltering Dwight, however. In his second start, a week later, he was sent out against the hot-hitting Chicago Cubs.

Ability is not enough: pitching is a thinking man's game. Here Gooden charts the pitches of a teammate so he will know how to pitch to these batters when it's his turn on the mound.

This time, Gooden learned the difference between Class A minor-league hitters and major-league veterans. The Cubs jumped on him for six runs and chased him to the showers before the fourth inning was over.

Devastated by the 11-2 loss, Gooden lost his confidence. His fastball had always been a mysterious gift; Dwight had never known why he could throw it so well. When he threw as he always had and was still hit hard, he couldn't help but wonder if the gift had left as suddenly as it had come. As he did after every game he pitched, Dwight called his dad. "Maybe I lost it," he worried. Once again, Dan Gooden calmed his son's fears. The next time Gooden struck out seven batters in five solid innings of work.

During the month of May, Dwight continued to bounce from success to failure. One day, he was shelled for eight runs in $2\frac{1}{3}$ innings by the Astros, and, five days later, he shut out the Los Angeles Dodgers on just four hits. As Gooden grew more comfortable in the major leagues, his confidence and competitiveness returned. Dwight remembered the cocky way the Cubs had acted when they had blasted him in that earlier 11-2 loss, and he could hardly wait to get back at them. When he got his chance, he beat them easily by a score of 8 to 1. Later, he pitched the best game of his career—a one-hitter—against those same Cubs.

By midseason, Gooden had been impressive enough to win a spot on the National League All-Star team.

On July 10, 1984, 19-year-old Dwight Gooden became the youngest player ever to enter an All-Star game. Whitey Herzog, the National League manager, did not give him an easy act to follow, however, as Fernando Valenzuela—perhaps the most famous young pitcher in the game—had just struck out all three American

Gooden (left) accepted the challenge of rival pitcher Fernando Valenzuela (above) in the 1985 All-Star game. After the Dodger lefty struck out the side in the fourth inning, Gooden did the same in the fifth.

League batters in the fourth inning. Now Gooden, an unknown talent to most American League fans, came in to face a string of power hitters.

The first to test Dwight was Detroit catcher Lance Parrish, who had already belted 16 home runs at the midpoint of the season. Gooden kicked his leg high and fired pitches that Parrish could barely see. The batter swung and missed at strike three. Next up was Tiger centerfielder Chet Lemon, batting .307 with 12 homers. Lemon never had a chance. He, too, never got a piece of the ball and went down swinging. Then Seattle's rookie sensation, Alvin Davis, tried his luck. Batting .280 with 18 home runs, Davis had been one of the hottest hitters in baseball. He coaxed two balls off the Met youngster but then he, too, hit nothing but air on a 2-2 pitch. The kid had struck out the side!

After those few minutes of work—plus another inning in which he allowed one hit but no runs—Dwight Gooden became baseball's newest celebrity. As reporters and fans flocked after him, the Mets again rushed to his rescue. They had learned from past experience what the crush of publicity could do to a young player. In 1980, when he had been proclaimed the best prospect in baseball, Met outfielder Darryl Strawberry had been left on his own to deal with the press, and the demands and frustrations had made it hard for him to perform for the team. Wiser this time around, the New York team hired a tutor to teach

Dwight how to handle interviews. They also screened interview requests and made Dwight available only after he had pitched.

The Mets let slugger Darryl Strawberry (right) sink or swim on his own in dealing with the press in his rookie season. After seeing the strain that was put on the right fielder, they tried a different approach with their next sensation.

The final part of the Mets' protective shield bothered Dwight to no end. In order to protect his valuable right arm from being struck by a pitch, they had Dwight switch from batting left-handed to swinging from the right side. Gooden had always taken pride in his hitting. In fact, he still insisted that, if given the chance, he would much rather play outfield than pitch. In one game, he had actually stroked three hits off Fernando Valenzuela. Having to bat right-handed would make it much tougher for Dwight to hit safely.

That season, Dwight Gooden proved to be the best bargain in baseball. Earning the minimum league salary of $40,000, he won 17 games, lost only 9, and finished second in the league in ERA with a 2.60 mark. But it was for his strikeouts that Dwight really became famous. For 73 years, Grover Cleveland Alexander had held the National League rookie strikeout record. Gooden buried Alexander's mark of 227 and then went on to shatter Herb Score's 29-year major-league record of 245.

By the end of the season, Gooden had chalked up 276 strikeouts in only 218 innings of work for an 11.39 average. Even the great Nolan Ryan had never averaged better than 10.57 strikeouts per 9 innings of pitching. No one could challenge Dwight in the voting for the National League Rookie of the Year. But along with his individual honors, Gooden also helped his club jump from last place to second in their division.

The rookie was not satisfied with his performance, however. He found a late-season game in which he struck out 16 Philadelphia Phillies and still lost, 2-1, especially hard to swallow. Gooden's downfall was that once a runner reached base against him, his high leg kick gave the runner a big jump in base stealing. Worse yet, he had allowed so few base runners in his career that he had never really learned how to hold them close to the base. At one point, 47 runners in a row had stolen against him without being thrown out. When the season was over, Gooden sought help to improve this flaw. After several weeks of work, he had managed to cut one-half second off his windup time and had developed a good pick-off move.

If Gooden had been spectacular in 1984, he was pitching in a world of his own in 1985. When he was scheduled to play, Met fans streamed to the park carrying cardboard squares with the letter *K* on them. (*K* is the baseball scorer's symbol for strikeout.) Whenever Dr. K—as Gooden was now known—got two strikes on a batter, the cheers, shouts, and foot stomping would practically shake the stadium. Batters must have felt the whole world was against them as they tried to hit the next searing pitch from the Doctor. More often than not, they would miss, and then an even louder howl would explode from the stands as the fans flashed their *Ks* in celebration.

With 9 "Ks" already chalked up, New York fans eagerly await
this two-strike pitch in hopes of recording number 10.

Baseball's trivia buffs started a countdown when Gooden aimed to become the youngest pitcher ever to win 20 games in a season. With 18 wins under his belt, Dr. K treated fans to a masterful performance in winning number 19. It was almost cruel to watch the serene-looking youngster turn an entire team of San Francisco Giants into helpless stick-wavers. Amid a sea of colorful *Ks* in the stands, Gooden struck out 16 Giants on his way to a seven-hit shutout.

The *Ks* were waiting for him again in his next start as Dr. K went for win number 20. It wasn't, however, quite the party atmosphere the fans would have liked. A steady drizzle made the ball hard to grip, and Dwight never did get into his usual rhythm. In fact, he nearly spoiled everything by giving the San Diego Padres two runs on a couple of wild pitches and a throwing error. Leading the game 4-3, Gooden left in the sixth inning for a pinch hitter. He had long been out of the game when Roger McDowell finished up to preserve his milestone 20th win. In 1939, 20-year-old Bob Feller had also won 20 games. But because he had been a month older than Dwight at the time, Dr. K owned yet another "youngest" record.

At the end of the season, Dwight earned one more record by an equally narrow margin. After leading the major leagues in wins (24 to 4 losses), earned run average (1.53), and strikeouts (268), Gooden was the unanimous winner of the National League's Cy Young Award.

Cy Young, the owner of the unreachable record of 511 wins, was a fitting choice as the namesake of the award that honors the best pitchers in the league.

Fernando Valenzuela had won the same award at age 21, but Dwight had received his three days before his 21st birthday.

Without Dwight's record, the Mets had managed only a 74-60 season. But with their awesome right-hander blazing away, they had chased the St. Louis Cardinals to the wire before being nosed out for first place. Dr. K kept the Mets close all summer by winning 14 straight games between May 30 and August 25. Perhaps the most impressive part of his season was the fact he had done it all while wearing an elastic brace on his right ankle to protect ligaments he had strained before the season had started.

Dwight Gooden so dominated the game that he became the most popular drawing card in sports. It became tougher and tougher for the Mets to shield him from all of the demands made on his time. For the most part, Dwight handled it all in the same calm, relaxed fashion he showed on the mound. Dodger ace Orel Hershisher pointed out that when you watched Gooden perform, you would think he was all by himself in the stadium instead of in front of thousands of screaming fans. Ignoring the crowds, Dwight would relax and go about his business without showing any emotion. Many believed this attitude was the key to his success on the mound as well as off.

Others thought they detected keys to Dwight's success in his powerful legs and unusually long fingers.

Although he seemed to have most situations well in hand,
Gooden could count on veteran catcher Gary Carter to lend a
steadying hand when necessary.

With his powerful kick off the mound providing most of the force for his pitches, Gooden didn't have to worry about straining his arm. His pitching motion was so smooth and coordinated that pitching coaches worried little that he would ever suffer the arm injuries that often plagued so many hard-throwing pitchers. And the fingers that were so long they seemed to swallow the baseball provided the extra snap to make his curve so effective.

What impressed older pitchers the most, however, was Dwight's knowledge of the game. In Dwight's phone conversations with his dad, he would go back over the game he had pitched, remembering what he had thrown to whom and where the pitch had gone. If he lost a game, he would tell his dad what had gone wrong and what pitch he should have thrown to the batter.

Again, there seemed to be no stopping Dr. K as he opened the 1986 season with his usual flawless form. Breezing through opponents for five straight wins, Dr. K ran his career record to an incredible 46-13. But gradually, the K-carrying New York fans found they weren't celebrating quite as before. Since he had never been as thrilled by strikeouts as the Met fans had been, Dwight had been working with pitching coach Mel Stottlemeyer on forcing batters into groundouts and pop-ups more easily. But as long as the fans could turn their attention to celebrating the Mets' surprising success, no one complained. By mid-June, New York was running away with their division, and Gooden was still coasting along with an impressive 8-2 record and a 2.11 ERA.

But as if a superhuman strength were slowly leaking out of him, Gooden slowly fell back into the ranks of the good National League pitchers. Slipping to 10-4 by midseason, Dwight lost the All-Star game by giving up a two-out home run to Detroit's Lou Whitaker. Then for awhile, nothing seemed to go right. In the sixth inning of a game against Houston, Dwight touched his hands to his mouth while on the mound, a violation of the "spitball" rules. He was penalized one ball on the count to Alan Ashby, who was not one of the Astros' stronger batters. The once unshakable Met ace ended up by walking Ashby to load the bases, and he was pulled from the game.

As frustrations mounted, advice poured in on "what was wrong with Doc." Actually, Gooden fought through the frustrations to post some fine statistics. He won 17 and lost only 6 with a 2.84 ERA, and he struck out 200 batters in 250 innings. But those weren't "Dr. K" caliber numbers. In fact, they weren't any better than the other three starters on the Mets' staff, so the criticism continued.

Some experts believed the frustration of the Houston series on top of a difficult season had shaken Gooden's confidence. When the Mets went to the World Series that year, Boston players thought he was trying to be too perfect with his pitches, and his pitching coach said that had prevented him from "getting into his groove."

It quickly became apparent, however, that Gooden's problems involved more than just his pitching technique. After a routine traffic citation exploded into a highly publicized scuffle with the Tampa police, rumors connecting him to drugs began to circulate—rumors that Gooden tried to dispel by offering to take a drug test. During spring training, while the one-time superstar was being hit hard by mediocre batters, those tests turned up the shocking evidence. Gooden had been using drugs.

Gooden's teammate Ron Darling once described pitching as "a roller coaster ride through the land of confidence." In his first three years as a pro, Dr. K had experienced a wilder ride than most. When he entered a drug treatment center, fans and friends wondered if the ride had come to a halt.

One month later, Gooden set about the task of regaining his lost reputation as a brilliant pitcher. Dwight would have to battle skeptical, even hostile, fans as well as his own doubts about himself. But after a few weeks of sharpening his skills in the minor leagues, Dwight Gooden returned to New York.

After the excitement of his early seasons with the Mets and then an agonizing struggle with drugs, Dwight had emerged as a more mature and stable person. In

1987, like the year before, Gooden was quietly effective. He led a late-season charge by the Mets that just fell short of catching the Cardinals in their division race. While setting a 15-7 mark, he led the Met starters in wins, earned run average, complete games, and shutouts.

Dwight came back even stronger in 1988, winning 18 games in New York's drive to the National League East Championship. In June of 1989, in a game against the Montreal Expos, he earned his 100th career win. Just 24 years old, he became one of the youngest players to reach this milestone. In 1990, Gooden appeared to be back in form with 223 strikeouts, his highest total in five years. The next year, Gooden was having a fine season. He posted his 132nd win (against just 53 losses) and carried a 13-7 season mark. Then a shoulder injury ended his season early. In September he had surgery to repair partial muscle tears, and he began the long process of recovery.

Gooden came back from the injury to pitch in 1992, but without the spectacular results he had given the Mets throughout his career. For the first time since he joined the major-league club, he posted a losing record at 10-13. Even so, he struck out 145 batters. The legendary "Dr. K" continues to pitch, trying to reclaim his place as an unstoppable force in the game of baseball.

DWIGHT GOODEN

Strikeout King

YEAR	TEAM	WINS	LOSSES	ERA	GAMES	INNINGS	HITS	Ks	WALKS
1982	Kingsport	5	4	2.47	9	$65\frac{2}{3}$	53	66	25
1982	Little Falls	0	1	4.15	2	13	11	18	3
1983	Lynchburg	19	4	2.50	27	191	121	300	112
1984	New York	17	9	2.60	31	218	161	276	73
1985	New York	24	4	1.53	35	$276\frac{2}{3}$	198	268	69
1986	New York	17	6	2.84	33	256	197	200	80
1987	New York	15	7	3.21	25	$179\frac{2}{3}$	162	148	53
1988	New York	18	9	3.19	34	$248\frac{1}{3}$	242	175	57
1989	New York	9	4	2.89	19	$118\frac{1}{3}$	93	101	47
1990	New York	19	7	3.83	34	$232\frac{2}{3}$	229	223	70
1991	New York	13	7	3.60	27	190	185	150	56
1992	New York	10	13	3.67	31	206	197	145	70

National League Play-offs

YEAR	TEAM	WINS	LOSSES	ERA	GAMES	INNINGS	HITS	Ks	WALKS
1986	New York	0	1	1.06	2	17	10	9	5
1988	New York	0	0	2.95	0	$18\frac{1}{8}$	10	20	8

World Series

YEAR	TEAM	WINS	LOSSES	ERA	GAMES	INNINGS	HITS	Ks	WALKS
1986	New York	0	2	8.00	2	9	17	9	4

Any time Dwight got two strikes on a batter, K-hungry fans at New York's Shea Stadium nearly shook the foundation with their stomping and howling.

ACKNOWLEDGMENTS: The photographs are reproduced through the courtesy of: pp. 1, 8, 23, 26, 28, 47, Ira Golden; pp. 2, 20, 30, 36, 44, UPI/ Bettman Newsphotos; pp. 6, 33, 40, George Gojkovich; p. 12, Thomas Donoghue; p. 15, California Angels; pp. 16, 31, Los Angeles Dodgers; p. 18, Hillsborough High School; p. 21, Montreal Expos; p. 25, New York Mets; pp. 38, 48, National Baseball Library, Cooperstown, N.Y.
Front cover photograph by Brian Yablonski
Back cover photograph by Jim Hathaway